Through

Screaming

Whispers

PROLOGUE

his brutally honest anthology relays the harrowing account of a slow and painful recollection of childhood torture suffered at the hands of sexual predators.

Trek through 6 years of undulating hell towards the light of change. Through the ravages of Complex Post Traumatic Disorder (C-PTSD), Extreme Anxiety and Depressive Disorders, you will get an insight into the workings of a broken mind, where trauma is unsure if it is present or past.

You will skirt the walls of tunnels within a mind of terror and a viewpoint of a toddler and emerge into the light, where change can begin. A tiny little girl awaits through screaming whispers cast onto dark walls with no ears.

This collective is also an insight into the current mental health crisis and care in the midst of what seems to be a pandemic of Lost Youth.

"Urgent Voices Scream,

Important Voices Whisper,

Contentment Needs no Voice,

and yet, Panic Has no Voice at all..."

Joelle Johnson

COPYRIGHT

"The decay of our heart

starts in the closet.

Through secret conversations

with God,

Screaming Whispers

fall like teardrops

as they unravel

and smudge

across the page.

These stains become

my poems of repair."

Joelle Johnson

DEDICATION

This Anthology is dedicated to the three people that have given me unwavering support through many years of intolerable, undulating paths of hell.

To my Clinical Psychologist, Paul Ward, thank you always for the safe place, quiet corners and comfortable couch. I could never repay your kindness, caring heart and availability. I miss our Iced Coffees and laughter—thank you for allowing the many venting emails written at midnight's distress.

To my Spiritual Counsellor, Justin, for your wisdom, guidance, cover in prayer and brother-ly love. Love you so much, my brother. Never a kinder heart. You're a good and faithful servant.

Talking about good and faithful servants to my most trustworthy friend, Jane, there are no words, just my tears. My gratitude reaches too deep.

CONTENTS

THE HUMAN

CONNECTION EXISTS

between TWO PEOPLE

when they feel

seen, heard, and valued;

when they can

give and receive

without judgement;

and when they

derive sustenance

and **STRENGTH** from the

relationship.

INTRODUCTION

*H*ow do you even begin an introduction to the heartache of this book? I do not know. I will say that poetry has always been a release for me and all my demons. It is the language that allows complete conflicting freedom, to which no rules in English apply. You can mix sensations with eerie pairings of words, you can jump all boundaries of time, and you can avoid the hard conversations by circling. It also suits the unveiling patterns of PTSD and allows the author to express snippets of images, tastes, sounds and smells.

No Barriers. No Rules. No Limits.

Writing in "poetry form" helped unearth memories stuck in my head from the torture of a toddler and the shadowless young girl hidden inside, both of which have long since separated, in my mind.

This work. It's not for the faint of heart.

Before we start, I just want to thank you for

hearing my story. I have found the traumas of the last six years are not something that can be shared with people that love you. The shame that it causes me, even at the thought of others knowing, is traumatic enough. So instead, I remain voiceless and sometimes have to endure criticism and judgment for my unexplainable actions.

Sometimes, people need to understand that they simply just don't understand, and in the lack of information, it should not be replaced with what *you think* is happening. Remember always; emotional understanding happens in your heart, not your mind. Guide your judgement to seek wisdom from your heart.

This world can be so obsessed with itself and not see both the beautiful, simple things in life or the countless many who have lost their way.

Seek out those that life has discarded

and love at least one of them.

I have shed many tears for people I see in pain, and as ill-equipped as I am, I have seen what is happening around me. If I can try, I hope we all can.

FOREWORD

by Paul Ward

I can imagine that two groups of people will find value in this anthology. Those who care for prose and literature will witness creativity borne from extreme trauma, leading to dark and distressing verses which describe unthinkable pain. The other group will be those who are fascinated by the human condition; they will note the transition from the early works which are full of confusion and chaos, through to the middle where anecdotes are shared of medication and hospitalisation that many of us will never experience. Finally, the later works are neat, rhythmic and organised, and possess a logical flow missing in the initial pieces. Whether you fit into the former or latter reader groups, or both, an understanding of the workings of the author's mind from a clinical perspective will be useful to you. It is such a perspective that I have been asked to offer. Following is a brief description of the key defence mechanisms and processes that have operated, primarily subconsciously, in the hidden recesses of our poet's mind over the past forty years.

In her 1969 book, "On Death and Dying", Elisabeth Kubler-Ross describes five stages of grief and loss: denial, anger, bargaining, depression and acceptance. These stages do not only apply to death; they are evident in victims of trauma where the loss refers to the loss of a feeling of safety and security, or the loss of innocence. The fear centre of the brain attempts to find a way to make sense of what has happened. If this can be achieved then the person can continue to feel that they live in a safe world where bad things do not happen to good people. Unfortunately we know all too well that we live in a world where bad things happen randomly and unpredictably, but no young child is able to cope with that reality.

Denial has been a primary coping strategy for our author since early childhood. Essentially, the fear centre of her brain has tried to assert that the trauma to which she was subjected never happened. Recall of trauma-related memories was blocked for decades. We often refer to this process as repression, or repressed memories. Unfortunately, repression is like trying to hold an inflated beach ball under the water in a swimming pool. Eventually it will pop up and slap you in the face. When repression breaks down, recall of memories is typically gradual and occurs bit by bit over an extended time period. This leaves the victim re-traumatised as each memory surfaces as if the abuse had just happened in the present day.

A second type of denial that can occur is when the brain decides that: 'the abuse did not happen to me, it happened to someone else'. This can lead to dissociation, which can sometimes take the form of an 'out of body experience'. The victim may feel that they are in a corner of the room, watching the abuse. Again, this is obviously totally false such as the assertion under repression that the abuse never happened. However, it is an effective short-term coping strategy when mere survival is the goal.

The bargaining stage can be just as illogical. Remember: the goal; is to make the victim feel that they live in a safe world where bad things do not happen to good people. So: 'if it *did* happen, I must not be a good person!'. The world is fair if bad things happen to bad people. This leads to cripplingly low self-esteem, as to feel safe the victim must believe that they deserved the abuse they received.

This bargaining process fits well with how anger must be accommodated. When a child is abused, the power dynamic is such that they cannot be angry at the perpetrator, who is typically older and/or stronger. The perpetrator will commonly groom the victim, stating that the child will not be believed if they tell anyone. This means that the victim feels that they cannot tell a caregiver, as the caregiver will be angry at them! As a result, the victim turns the anger inwards on themselves. The bargaining leads to them believing that they are a bad person, so they become angry at themselves for being bad and causing the abuse, reinforcing the low self-esteem even further. They do not feel that they deserve affection, and human touch becomes unwelcome.

It is easy to see how the victim becomes depressed, feeling that they are an awful, abuse-worthy person, and not even remembering the abuse which may explain why they are beset by these dark thoughts and feelings. Without the knowledge that the person was abused, even the finest therapist would struggle to put together the pieces of the puzzle and make sense of the inner dynamics of the client's mind.

When I first met the author, I saw a remarkable woman who had achieved much in her life including being a fine parent, but who mysteriously had extremely high levels of self-loathing. Initially our work centred on questioning whether this self-loathing was deserved, but it was not until her mind felt safe enough to start loosening its hold on her traumatic memories that we were able to construct a working model of how her thoughts were interacting. We are now striving towards acceptance, the final stage in the aforementioned model.

We can witness the transition through these stages in the poems in this anthology. The initial writings talk of shame, and anger turned inwards. For example, in 'Never Enough':

'I crave for human touch, but cannot accept it'

'I will never be enough for me; Nor will I ever be enough for others'

The splitting of the personality and dissociation I had directly referenced in 'Three Points of View' which describes the trifurcation eloquently:

'I feel a cleaving in my mind; As my brain is simply split;
The corridors of memory; Between myself and it'

We then witness the reality of what has happened leaking through as the defence mechanism of denial and repression breaks down. From 'Obscurity':

'My ever-decreasing cage; Of dark captive thoughts'

And later in the same poem the author refers to:

'the war that is my mind'

The war is between repression, and logical acceptance.

The sad truth for our author is that there is not a perfect victory awaiting her at the end of this process. What awaits her is acceptance of the awful truth that she was subjected to some of the most dehumanising, complex and sustained abuse I have come across in all my years of practice. When I read the final poem: 'Bring Her Home', I can only help but wonder whether it speaks of hope, or of the end of hope. Yes, the now-consciously accessible bad memories will be counterpointed by a knowledge that she was not to blame, that she should not feel guilty or ashamed, and that she is a good person, but that will never be enough to take away the pain of what she has experienced. That is why I admire her efforts to make the best of her life and to persevere, and I will continue to do what I can to show her that she is cared for and loved, and that she is a valid and valuable person.

Paul Ward, Clinical Psychologist, Perth Western Australia, February 2022.

NOTE FROM THE AUTHOR

I ENCOURAGE you to read both the **FORE-WORD** and the **REVIEW** on this book before you delve in, thus gaining further context and warning for its contents. Neither will take away from the experience of the book, no spoiler alerts or any such thing, just context.

Both are listed in the contents for location.

CHAPTER 1

Chasing Bunnies

J didn't lose my mind; the truth is, it got shit scared and ran away to chase a bunny. By the time it realised the bunny was dead, it was all too late. That's pretty much what losing my mind looked like. A frenetic chase of altered realism. It's funny; well, it has to be because the truth is damn near terrifying.

When you look back on your life, you can often see the precise moment that the unhinging took place. However, for me, it felt like bits were dropping off for months. I guess that is the sneaky working of C-PTSD.

In a recent moment of meditative practice, I asked myself a question that seemed far too complex to answer.

"Would you prefer not to know? We will get to the answer to that question further on in the book.

In the meantime, I hear my mother's voice, "You have some explaining to do, young lady!".

It was not until much later in life did I discover that almost everything in my memory from childhood was masking the most unimaginable trauma. Over the space of six years, these traumas have unfolded through careful navigation by a specialised PTSD Clinical Psychologist and my rock of strength. I don't know where I would be today without him.

In short, I was a competent, intelligent, meticulous woman. Within three months, I could barely work, I lost my husband, and then I lost my mind.

This book picks up from there and is a collection of poems written through the journey of

discovering these memories and the conse-
quent unveiling, year after year, the sexual tor-
ture of a toddler. I had countless moments
under my belt of a brutality that is hard to de-
scribe. My set of traumas is so deep that it is
not wise to share with non-professionals. It is
simply unimaginable. Only two or three of my
friends know my life; the rest, heck, they sus-
pect I have a few screws loose! They judge me
for my peculiarities, too.... yeah.. that's another
book. In all fairness, I don't correct them. I
can't.

Don't worry. I have only given you the cup-
cake version here. You'll be ok. If not, know
that I will be, eventually. I am in great hands.

I have a very curious mind. It loves to learn.
All manner of things take my interest. It is
simply fascinating from boat building to history,
from paper manufacture to exploration tunnels,
and the mind itself and its corridors of unchar-
tered territory.

These poems are in chronological order. It is
interesting to watch the deterioration of the
mind, the explosions of the truths, the sheer
head in the sand denial and the final heart-

break of resignation. You see, I write these poems as part of the release out of my head, so it happens mostly without consciousness. I don't generally read them once written, so having to sit and read, collate and absorb them again, I realised they formed a story, a progression if you will, and to me, it is fascinating how that has unfolded when put into book form. So let's get into it.

The first thing I lost was the ability to touch. Being an extrovert, it was a challenging time.

NEVER ENOUGH

Some crave time alone.

Some long for peace and quiet.

There are some, like me,

who are still utterly alone

even within a room of people.

I crave for human touch, but cannot accept it
I crave unguarded conversation, but cannot al-
low it
I crave devotion, but have never obtained it
I crave parental love, and never received it
I crave my child's acceptance and have lost it

I have what others wish for,

yet die within its boundaries.

The confinement of being with and within the
only person you truly despise,

Immersed in their thoughts,

wrapped in their disdain of you,

and trapped by shame,

there is no separation of soul and self for me.

I will never be enough for me.

Nor will I ever be enough for others.

SUBMERSION

The horn blasts

A call to retreat

As darkness seeps through closed eyelids

Cannot contain

Cannot restrain

The beast within.

OBSCURITY

A cruel darkness hovers
A blanket of fear descends
My lifeless will limps
To a meagre whisper from the deep

The surrounding sounds muffle
As it beats to close me in
My ever-decreasing cage
Of dark captive thoughts

Arrows of insults
Pierce, my very soul
Fuelling a fire
Already burning too bright.

No Escape, no retreat
As each voice has a turn
At my conscious belief
Pummelling it into reality

Talons from my fingers
Gouge desperation on walls
From clawing tunnels
Of the war that is my mind

I fight to stand and hold my ground
And the floor is ripped away
Down to the cold, dank floor
Again... down we go.

I can't fight. I can't argue
I can't lay a stake in my claim
No me is left in this darkness
No anything to save

The blood still flows
Through lifeless forms
And I scurry and scream
To a place with no doors.

I know my worth is nothing
I know my air is wasted
I know my heart is tired
I know my soul still longs

Joelle Johnson

Reach down your hand further
I can't meet you halfway
Reach down your hand further
Or take me away.

CHAPTER 2

The Reckoning

*B*attling with depression is a force to be reckoned with. At this point, I was slowly losing my independence, confidence, and will to live. I could not understand the story that was playing out in my head. I could make neither head nor tail of the truth. The hatred I felt towards my incompetence to deal with my issues was spiralling fast, and the battle with suicide and hospitalisation began.

You cannot help but notice the reality of an epidemic of depression in mostly young adults suffering from all manner of grief. It hits home as I watch them ravage themselves to death in anguish, fighting a cause they no longer can even identify.

When running circles in the mental health lifestyle, you start seeing a life you have absolutely no comprehension exists. It is one hell of an eye-opening experience.

To clarify, my inferences of medications in the following poems do not look favourably at them as a tool to help. That is no longer my opinion; they are almost imperative with trauma. However, at this stage of my story, I got very frustrated watching these people fall apart at the seams from within the walls of the most acute Mental Health Wards in my state.

DEPRESSION

Gut-wrenching solo journey

Within the midst of despair

Wrapped in weighted sorrow

The heart of the devil's snare

Waking, invisibly swaddled

Pressing and holding you down

Seeping sadness through you

Waiting until you drown

You cannot move
The effort hard to find
Laden down by black
My body was not mine

The absence of thought
The ramping of feelings
The mind shuts off
And sensory comes squealing

Held firmly under
A raging wispy ocean
Swirling claws of dread
As hell is set in motion

Dizzied by a hypnotic loss
As voluntary motion cuts
The light of life fades
As the path, out, shuts.

A swirling endless struggle

For the reaches of your soul

Tortured without mercy

Consuming its victim's whole

No escape from hopelessness

As it's splitting at your seams

With deafly silent screaming

So loud, it echoes in your dreams

THE FORGOTTEN

Amidst the raging speed of life

Decisions thick and fast

The sad, the lost, the broken

Are pushed aside or passed

The acuity of listening

A skill long since lost

The hurting, troubled soul

Shall pay the final cost

The cookie-cutter response

Comes many shades and sizes

In milligrams and Capulets

The drug response just rises

So out comes the subscription

A pill for this and that

And let's not forget

The drug to counteract.

Before too long, the days are short

Stumbling in a doped demise

The nights give way to robust ways

To stop the patient's cries

I'm not my diagnosed acronym

So don't medicate my letter

Don't oppress me with your pills

These steps don't make me better

Two ears are needed

With more than a brief talk

Mix that with understanding

And teach me how to walk

Your drugs are just a hindrance

And cause all sorts of strife

Twisted reality distortion

Will slice you like the knife

Life is full of problems

With stressors left and right

Why don't you take the time

To teach me how to fight.

Joelle Johnson

THE MADHOUSE

The silent halls arise

The shuffling sheets stir

From drug-induced silence

With zombie eyes a blur

Hyper teen shrieks

Bouncing from her bed

Where she cried herself to sleep

While beating at her head

Doleful cutter sniffs

Sedated from the blade

Relief no doubt subsiding

From new lines, she has laid

These walls here, they talk
And become so very kind
To a woman who is conversing
With someone in her mind

She shuffles slowly, scuffing
Her pretty little slippers
As she finds another hallway
And huddles up the *nippers

The silent little manipulator
Awakes to play the game
To get a daily drug fix
Using anything to blame

But even if there's nothing wrong,
There's certainly something there
As why on earth would you choose
To be inside this horrendous snare

The shared zone is bustling

As the rooms are closed for cleaning

The addition of testosterone

Have anxieties reeling

The men you see are hungry

Always looking for some food

Feeding is a frenzy

to subdue the foggy mood

The line has already started

From the kitchen slot

Waiting, impatiently scratching

To see what they have got

The voice of angels opens

With the doors of the lady's wing

But how that sweet voice changes

As her drugs being too thin

When the breakfast is clear

I return to my room

Where cutter is still sleeping

And will remain until noon

Again we start the dance

Of the lunch from the slot

And more the tempers flaring

From the men amongst the lot

Hairy belly angry man

With his yellow shirt too short

You see his belly heaving

As his nostrils flair and snort

The lunch that he has ordered

Isn't what he found

Ensues a rage that has him

Stamping his feet upon the ground

The aggression has me frightened

Running to my room

As I hear the others taunting

Big belly man's boom

Mixing among the commotion

Doctors, nurses, security

All in different corners

Trying to offer some surety

Now the panic alarm has sounded

The cutter has hung herself again

The Code Blue is shouted

Her body lifted off by men

The shower is still running

And filling up the floor

Their knees are swiftly skidding

As they pump her chest once more

There is no honest answer

No end to the commotion

Just balance like a circus

Constantly in motion

How is this the answer

These kids are so young

Has society just failed them

Their life has yet begun.

nippers (Slang) little children

Joelle Johnson

CHAPTER 3

The Good, The
Bad & The Ugly

*I*t seems the further I dig a hole towards despair; eventually, a hand reaches down to pull me out. My Jesus. My Faith. How hard a woman holds to the promise of love. The will to live never once returned without the company of the cross for me. It's time to revisit that question from the meditative moment. That question seemed far too complex to answer on first pondering.

"Would you prefer not to know?".

If I had a choice never to find out my past, I would not take it, primarily because of God. That suffering draws me to the cross. In that, I mean when you are in the depths of despair, and it is almost unbearable to be alone there, you discover the comfort of Christ. The reassurance that He knows suffering and can reach you for it. I would not trade that precious gift for any suffering to pass my door. I don't say I am a Christian; I simply love God. It has to be that simple for me. I have to love him in my private way. He is a part of who I am. I don't fit the traditional mould of Christianity; I don't like churches because of the noise, so I don't attend; I am not a gentle, rational, or wonderful person that thinks only for the service of God. I have nothing to share towards my faith with others, not at the moment; I have a wicked sense of humour; I swear, and most of the time, I think of death. So not traditional, but God knows all of me, and I am sure, He understands me, even when others don't. That is the truth of how I suffer daily.

The closing thing here, it breaks my heart that I cannot be who I am. I cannot explain why I want to die because my friends are not emotionally equipped to handle this truth. So I come across as irrational, stupid and selfish. I have to wear that judgement to retain my privacy. I would rather be all of those things to others than be swallowed in shame.

Nevertheless, as this journey continues, I am growing tired of this unveiling of memories in my mind. The pain is indescribable. The dredging out of dreams makes me feel like I am shedding skin — those horrific bastards. I want to be angry, but I know hurt people, hurt people. I have to walk towards forgiveness because no other alternative exists.

It is for yourself for those who do not truly understand what forgiveness is. For no one else. By letting go, genuinely releasing the person/s of their debt to you, then you can detach from the pain of their betrayal. Your heart can then be free to repair. This does not mean that I understand what happened and why. I know the truth of it is, I was just unlucky. At least that is the drum that Paul has beaten for years. I know, in my mind, that is true, but it would be great if someone would explain it to my heart.

LISTLESS

Is there anything more listless

Then to witness a soul travel

On the tides of time

Having abandoned hope?

Floating randomly between

A demand of the heart

And a relentless assault

Of sinful interruption.

Even the great Paul*

Willing in spirit,

Knew betrayal of the flesh was near

And cautioned us.

Love called us out in purpose

He wants to ruin our hearts

For anyone but Him

To love and to follow.

He calls us out from dark doors

And cold, dank tunnels

to take our breath

From the walls of His lungs

Drawing out the very life

Sustained by the purpose of his hope.

*Biblical Reference – Apostle Paul

ENTER THE DOORS

I can't fight.

I can't argue

I can't lay a stake in my claim

Nothing is left in this darkness

Nothing to save

The blood still flows

Through lifeless forms

And I scurry and scream

To a place with no doors.

I know my worth is nothing

I know my air is wasted

I know my heart is tired

I know my soul still longs

Reach down your hand further

I can't meet you halfway

Reach down your hand further

Or take me away.

Joelle Johnson

A POET'S CONSIDERATIONS

Words stumble and trip

The intent lost in idle chat

Some emotions need more

Of a poets consideration

Dredging up sentiments

That stick to the walls of

A crowded mind of fear

Dripping neatly in one line

Refusing to let go, let loose.

Caged beasts bare gnarly teeth

To unwanted disturbances

All the while dripping gums

Merge into lost bladders

As they fight to remain captive

Where predictions are known

Oh, too are doors slammed

On memories of blood pooling

Vomiting on copper collected in taste

Hair matted and clumped

With pure angst and apprehension

Hands imprinted by thick-soled shoes

Legs battered and bruised

By coarse strands of rope and

Kicks, like rubbish, is tossed

With pain so unimaginable

Even this poet has no words

With which to describe.

Locked, pinned down in a hall

Where displayed proudly

On clinker brick walls

These items of terror

Found usually mundane

In every home

Now evoke a panic of comprehension

knowing what they are

And yet understanding

They will be adapted for new use

At the hands of barbarous

Fiends with no mercy

A child's inconceivable

Disturbed scream

Normally conjures any parent

To action by their side

Not this girl though

Locked so so deep

In a corridor with no end

She waits for the visions

Of her mother to pass

As she eagerly listens nearby

To pain yelled so loud

From the walls of her daughters

undeveloped lungs.

A betrayal, so unimaginable.

What did I do?

How do you stand to hear

Me scream for you

I cannot look to the smile

Upon your face

Or the money in your hands

I do not need to see it

It haunts me every night.

That sound is swallowed whole

In a moment of your next breath

you take it in your stride.

I love you, mummy

I'll be better next time.

I love you, mummy

Rest now; it's too late for you.

Where can I go in these places

Where can I find the rest

I forgive my mother. Hurt People, Hurt People.

I cannot imagine her pain;

what happens to a mother that makes her do this?

Don't judge her.   You don't know her story, and neither do I.

CHAPTER 4

The Three in One

*R*ight, I usually joke about this complex brain distortion I have. But today, I feel great shame to reveal this to the world through this word. I don't like having screaming voices inside of me; they wake me up, they keep me from sleeping, they need so much from me, as children do.

I wrote the following poem to unravel what this 3 in 1 is in my mind. I do not hear physical voices, more an inference of them. The first one, "The Little One", I see as a screaming child, mouth wide, eyes popping out with distress and tension, but the audio button is off.

So, the inference of noise is there. The complexity of not hearing makes it worse to bear. I also have an almost photographic memory, video roll, smell, and acute sensation recall, or maybe it is not a photographic memory, I concede that due to the pain and violence, mixed with the intricate details of the memory, that it just feels like a real-life video roll.

I can only describe the "second child" as a shrivelled-up mess, unable to do anything but watch the events unveil themselves. She is meek. She is frail. She hovers in the corner of the ceiling. She is black, not like the colour, but more a representation of consumption. She squirms in posture always as if feeling a constant crawling sensation on her skin. She is Consumed in pain, fear and apprehension.

I get mad at both of them. One single event may play in three rolls of "film". We start as the "Little One". The view switches to the ceiling to the "Second Child" when a sensory overload happens. Then I have *my* memory of "rediscovering that memory" to deal with, which is also very traumatic. The other dimension I also have is being a mother. Processing the shock of watching that happen to a child. It seems impossible to deal with all of these things together. They have to be addressed one at a time. Each circle around the collective issues reveals a new perspective or understanding, making it seemingly impossible to deal with completely. My problems now are that I don't see either of those children "are" me. Mentally I know they are, but my heart will have no bar of it. To accept it as fact is accepting the dysfunction of my family and so many other things that I refuse to investigate. It's like denial is a river in Egypt.

Continuing the journey, the inhabitation of the two "others" is becoming intense. They want something off me. I do not know what. I still don't understand it. If you have not read the Foreword, Paul explains it from his Clinical perspective. I define it way differently. At this point in the journey, they simply piss me off. Much like people judge me for my suicidal ideations, no one knows of my struggles. But they judge me anyway.

THREE POINTS OF VIEW

I feel a cleaving in my mind
As my brain is simply split
The corridors of memory
Between myself and it

The rising of my stomach
And the contents there within
Have given way to one of three
The first of which gave in

The tiny defenceless child

Who screams most every night

A harrowing call for help

From the dark towards the light

She's trapped, the little one

Swaddled in a blanket of fear

Still looking towards her mum

Begging to be held dear.

The corridor is open now

To the second child within

Diffident in nature as she

Watches the happening

Tortured, she has split

From pain too much to bear

She left the poor child alone

Screaming without air

Burrowed tight within a corner

Perched high up in the air

Unreachable, unseeable

But her penance is to stare

Now a shell is left all broken

A person shamed and scattered

Way too many pieces

Is the third, this one the hazard

The potential for displacement

As the doors are yanked ajar

Peering eyes are seeking

The memories from afar

Oh triple observation

Can you stop the wheel in motion

Turn it counterclockwise

And erase the very notion

Joelle Johnson

Tell me what I did that day

That made them take her coat

Then guide my three-year-old self

To slit her little throat

IN THE MIDST OF SORROW

In the midst of sorrow

I found unrecoverable joy

Swallowed whole by sexual thuggery

And disposed of like a toy.

The porous heart of a child

Draws into its foundation and core

Fear with no exemption

and the shame of a dirty whore

When will these trespasses stop

On the surface of recollection

Thick sludge, encapsulated darkness

With no path toward objection

How much? How much? HOW MUCH!

Dark torment to bare

Gasping, drowning and reaching,

Clambering towards the air

Oh wretched hurt engross

Guttural cries of pain linger

While heavy heeled boots

Hold captive toddlers' fat fingers

Open mouth and empty screams

To hear a reassuring, "it's ok."

Prodding, poking and scampering

Little legs are tied, and splay

Wake hurried to tearless throat

And panicked, scurried terror

Gasping, confused and alone

Feeling it's all your error

How lonely the night calls

For numbers not spoken

For those to share the burden

Of a child utterly broken

Why is my burden so quiet

Contorted within my being

And others don't see MY choice

Of cutting loose and freeing?

Have they lived through such betrayal!

How dare they have the gall!

If they saw inside my memories

They would let me end it all.

CHAPTER 5

Please No More

*D*o you know where your limit is? Have you had the experience, as I am sure we all have, where you fall to your knees and cry "why" or "please no more"—that limit of sinful interruption? That limit for me has been undulating in severity for the last two years, where nothing seems to be working to ease the terror of life enough for me to proceed.

I am disturbed by the thought of leaving my adult child to the world alone. That used to be the motivation to keep putting one step in front of another, but these last years have stagnated in change. You just remain haunted by the things that clog your memory, paralysed by what seeps into the dream world and petrified by the simpleness of living. I feel that I am losing more each day, and then something miraculous will happen, and I get a few steps forward. However, each one of those slips backwards tears another layer from my armour. Each one, after recovery, I find I am more delicate.

The thing with the memories, when you are stuck with them replaying for months, if not years, is you become so familiar with them, and yet, it doesn't dull the experience. If anything, it enhances it. I wonder if that is because I don't deal with it, I don't speak it out, I don't grieve?

When I sat to write the Broken Heart poem, I was trying to write about one particular incident; however, later, reading it back, it is a culmination of several different memories. I noticed that some of those details span across almost all memories.

The details, I guess to psychological treatment, may be irrelevant, but it's the devil in the details for me.

A toddler is walking down the stairwell to a basement of torture. One side of the stairs has no railing, and the other is the clinker brick wall. The haunting singularly zoomed in on a tiny little hand, chubby little fat fingers that toddlers have, flowing over the undulating bricks as they jut out from the walls. That "scene", seemingly harmless to anyone but me. Just from the hand, I see the angst, terror, trepidation, agony and the most intense fear as an adult to watch.

A child. Imagine feeling all of that, but not knowing, not having the vocabulary to name this, or the mind to argue with this, or authority to voice anything and rely only on what sensations you feel inside your body. A child knows fear, happiness, and pain, but they are helpless to move beyond that boundary of those rudimentary feelings.

Fortunately for me, there are not many Clinker Brick walls around anymore, but I find being in the presence of this inanimate object raises a fear in me that is directly from the Little One. She screams through whispers which contorts my insides until my body wants to faint or vomit from the overwhelming sensations twisted and contorted within my stomach.

The poem "Why" is an argument between suicide and survival. An impossible argument. Don't be mistaken at the thought that these are both choices. Survival has not been an attractive choice for a long time, and now I have replaced suicide with Pride. Not a very Christian thing to do, but it can be used to your advantage when you are as stubborn as I.

The majority would call cowardice or selfishness at an untimely end to my life. This is where the power of Pride comes in. I am not a coward. I have never been. I do not shy away from trouble. Neither am I selfish. I think, as we all do, we have moments of it and periods in our adolescence that are rife with selfishness, but as a whole, it is not a word that the two or three that know me would use. (at least I hope so) and yet, for all eternity, I will be labelled with gossiping whispers literally from the benches of my own funeral, from those that love me, as a "selfish coward". Will it matter to me when I am dead? No. But is that what you want to leave with your child?

I have people in my life right now that harm me with their thoughtless responses. Acting to others as if they know what is happening, filling the blanks with lies and deception, talking about things they do not know. These people are friends. I know they mean no malice; I know they do not have wretched hearts, but they do not see that statement I made at the beginning of this book, that "in the absence of understanding, not to fill that hole, with what you **think** to be true".

So when my child comes past them one day, after I am gone, knowing them as their mothers' loved and seemingly trusted friends, what will they offer to him? What fabrication will my child receive? How will they punctuate my life in a paragraph as they reminisce to him? Don't tell me they will not want to say something that will ensure it is not his fault and that your mother was.....

You may say that this isn't an accurate response. "Would people do that?" I have to tell you, sadly yes.

After death, I have been at the receiving end of this type of machination. I had a mutual friend of the deceased person stop me in a shopping centre, and confront me, offloading a hoard of pure lies, in a nasty screaming defence of how I behaved after the person died. All done at the instigation of another's words. You did this, and that—all of the accusations belonged to another. I stood there, hands over the ears of my then young child, and had to listen and watch as other shoppers around just gawked at what a wretched horrid person I was. It is darn near impossible to be 100% clear in innocence in an argument; I was unequivocally innocent on every single account. Is it the woman's fault? Not really; she is just acting on what whispers left behind. Her delivery could do with some significant improvement though.

Now I am not saying that I am in any way perfect, or I never speak out of turn, or I never say things I don't mean, but I tell you one thing for sure. I have some great friends who will pick me up on wrong actions and, with love, they make sure I know the error of my ways. I am glad about that. I will take accountability when

I am aware of what I have done. I will try to rectify the behaviour. And like everyone else, I will fall again. I know I do this because I always seem to be apologising to someone.

So this leaves me with only one choice when I have only one consideration, my child.

Words do not teach your truth. It is actions alone that teach your children who you are.

I love him as much as I can so that he is never in doubt of his worth and value to my heart, and that will let him know that he has no accountability in my final result.

MY BROKEN HEART

Broken little dreams

Carved nicely in the sand

As fierce unfettered men

Take you by the hand

School uniform discarded

To don a pretty dress

Lacey socks and patent shoes

Pretty girl impress

Standing atop concrete stairs

As terror now consumes

Little fat fingers glide

On the surface of the room

A basement full of torture

The goal to dominate

Inflict pain and terror

Any means to humiliate

Brittle stickers cover

Wounds of my duress

Purple ribbons close

Slices of distress

Overstretched sleeves

Hide fearful clenched hands

Smiley faces mask

Fiercely violent plans

All of it is a cover

Or maybe a twisted game

Don't let them know you

They may unravel the shame

Pack down the troubles

Swallow the woes

Hide it! Hide it!

So nothing shows

Somewhere in that deception

The accuracy is shot

And all that is left

Is something I am not.

With no real foundation

Or basis of my being

I've forgotten who it is

I'm supposed to be freeing

Alas, linger and look inside

Reveals all the mystery

There's nothing inside

But blood awful history

WHY

The why of all my questions

Is weighing down a vacancy

Within the midst of misery

Where answers hit complacency

This driven understanding

Has torn apart a soul

And considers in its residency

To consume my life whole

Maybe the "why" I'm chasing

Has no real resolve

What if I stop running?

Will this question just dissolve?

Instead, I pose another

To ask just of me

Why are you considering

To leave your "why" and see?

It does not excuse my doings

And the print it will leave behind

To the only one who loved me

And this broken, twisted mind!

CHAPTER 6

Making Peace

I'm not a psychologist, and I have no comprehension of how healing comes about. What is the secret pathway? Who knows what steps are next towards recovery? I am not usually the one that handles that worrying. It belongs to the professionals and is on a much higher pay grade than I could comprehend. However, I equally concede that sometimes the sensors in your body rule and overtake your mind in what it needs next. They demand to be identified and given a voice, and this beautiful sensation of love is now at the forefront and ready to take charge.

Through a terrifying but deeply personal organic process, I am moving forward now. I've spent the best part of the last few years trying to kill off, silence, and muzzle the cries of those two within. It was the only option I had. The concept of embracing them is beyond comprehension, as I feel so very inept.

How do you hold <u>that</u> child? Physically? Mentally? Emotionally? I can't do any of it.

The grief of that embrace terrifies me. It will be the most painful thing I will have to do. In Paul's wisdom, or by chance – he would say wisdom - he guided me to switch to another very skilled professional, and the fact that she is female, I think, will be the saving grace for this next task.

Regina is another Clinical Psychologist and very specialised in Mindfulness-Based Cognitive Therapy and some other trauma-based therapies. She has a highly peace-seeking nature. She is incredibly gentle. I think Paul and I chose her, subconsciously, for the "Little One" locked inside. Or maybe even the "Little One" chose her for herself?

Nevertheless, Regina will be passionately present for her. I want to say that I wrote this poem for Regina. But oddly, maybe not.

This poem came to me in a melody, a rocking, swaying and floating piece of music. I had it "humming" in my mind trying to work out what it was for? I didn't think for one minute it was a poem.

This simply fell to the page with effortless fluidity when I sat to write next. It was like a dream. Even when I read it and hear the words within my heart, it plays like a song. It makes me smile through tears as I imagine the "Little One" holding her teddy and listening to me read to her, slowly changing her gaze from sadness to an overwhelming sense of acceptance while she wraps her chubby little fingers around my neck. Come to think of it, maybe it's more accurate to call it a Lullaby. I believe it is the sweetest I have ever heard.

BRING HER HOME

I hear "The Little One" approaching
       toward my ear.
Her tiny heart is sighing,
in the basement, she is lying,
oh, so soon she will be dying,
       in my ear.

Oh, I wish I could help you
       before you go.
On a day when all alone,
I would bring you to my home,
just to see how much you have grown,
       before you go.

I hope that I may greet you
>   with a kiss.

I close my arms as you resisted,

flooded with tears, I assisted,

to show a love that's not twisted,
>   with a kiss.

You sat there right beside me
>   Little One.

I felt your heart now settled,

among my flesh, you simply nestled,

away from a world you never settled,
>   Little One.

But I see the slumber's fear,
>   frightened child.

Now consoled you are sleeping,

holding, wishing you were keeping,

from that cry so simply weeping,
>   frightened child.

In the morning, as its sun
       softly shines,
In the mirror, we are one,
can we manage just to run,
toward the light as the sun,
       softly shines.

Not a drop of morning dew,
       never one!
Fresh air as senses started,
all the fear is simply parted,
but I watched her broken-hearted,
       in the sun.

My desire has only ever been,
       one with you!
Though my abilities, they forsake me,
into a world, they will take me,
no matter what, I cannot make me,
       one with you.

So let's take you to Regina

      Little One.

Wherein time, she may lift us,

and all-loving she will sift us,

Through a world that will drift us,

      back as one.

CHAPTER 7

In Closing About the Author

I debated writing this section so much so, that I sit and write it now, only weeks away from my publication date.

If I had read this book, I would want to know if "she" was ok. So it's from that standpoint I pace the lounge dictating through my headset to you now in an "About the Author" merged "Chapter 7" extra.

I want to convey many things, but the reality is that life is still a struggle. It is getting better, but more in a "three steps forward, two back" kind of way.

For years, I thought I would resolve my issue with diligent and skilful care, but it seems so far-fetched a dream now that I find myself halfway into a place of quiet resignation where I can attempt to make some good out of what has happened.

I'm lucky that I have not had a moment in these years where there was no one to go to. That in itself is a miracle. I am blessed with one very core group of friends that just love me through all my insanity.

In hospitals, I have had countless hours with people who almost forget the art of communication through the lack of it. It breaks my heart to think that having *"no one to talk to is translated in their mind that they are not worth talking to!"* That's a huge difference like, not being loved doesn't make you unlovable. But that is the translation that plays in their minds. It's hard work on them.

I don't have idle, unmeaningful chats; honestly, I don't think I can do it. I'm really intense. I challenge my thoughts, conversations, and understanding of what I hear most of the time. I'm not saying that I am the ultimate communicator; that would be a gross falsehood, but I do try to be, and I think that is the point. I think they matter; I believe they are lovable.

Simply put, I feel their pain when I am near them. It seeps through with such anguish and needs. It awakens the human connection in me. I have seen all manner of pain and sadly am well versed with it. But that can become your friend.

I will say that when I take "retreats" from life, I spend so much time with the person I hate. Me! It is a complex and panic-ridden experience for the most part. If I had a counterbalance to the devil that is in my ear, I might be much better off, but alas, that angel fell a long time ago, broke his leg and a wing in the fall and has never returned to my other shoulder.

I can't say I ever started with an ego anyway, so I don't miss it. It's safe expecting nothing of yourself. I huddle to that safety to just get through my day. I'm trying to change that attitude though. It's a process.

Let me also make room for an exceptional course that I have just finished. It would be remiss of me not to mention this, especially considering the audience this book may reach, and tell you what I learned to be most beneficial, aside from therapy, to my Mental Health.

I have been studying MBCT (Mindful Based Cognitive therapy), which, to be fair, I approached with trepidation. It's not my thing. So you can imagine my surprise when I got results so fast, and it has been a life-changer for me. I wanted to bring that up because if you also suffer from Trauma, Anxiety, or any other Depressive Disorder, Mindfulness is a force to be reckoned with. I would, however, throw caution in here first to seek out a professional MBCT Program. It trains you from a purely cognitive foundation, and a Clinical Psychologist is also taking you through with caution and skilful care. I promise you; it will be money well spent. Please give it a go.

I have a half plan to write an autobiography, and I will begin when this is published. Even though most of it was already written in the poems, this book has still been very cathartic to process. I feel a little stronger, so I think I can manage the book. However, I will be mindful of my reactions and stop when I need to re-group. So let's see.

I do want to close this section with a plea.

Over the last two years, and I assume, because of the pandemic, the "lost" have come to the forefront for me.

We all have our soapbox topic, and mine is the Broken Hearted. The youth that I have spent many hours talking to. Paradoxically, also the older generation of men that are homeless with mental health issues.

This heartbreak is palpable in a hospital setting. Gosh, I do wish that people could experience it.

I am holding so close to my heart of late the NEED to see what is happening around me; how can I do one thing to help.

There is so much need for care, concern and love without judgement in our society. I would not have guessed that I would be so obsessed with doing my bit to love people at this juncture in life. Me, the one who cannot be touched.

The unlovable one. The one who hates so very richly towards herself.

I cannot explain that, but I allocate those self-thoughts to my trauma. They are not me. That is not what I stand for in life.

Let me close this journey with a rude awakening for me and a deciding factor to write this last chapter.

As a patient, I was recently in a Mental Health Ward, and under duress, as with everyone else there. Two older men in the ward were both homeless, and I am humiliated to say they annoyed me so much. One gentleman was fascinated with a need to collect and re-purpose rubbish. He would turn an old plastic coke bottle into a flower, a straw into the stem, and cut slithers shaped like leaves from the green yoghurt containers. Mountains and mountains of trash, he sat and meticulously re-purposed these things to bring others joy and life to something discarded. It honestly annoyed the hell out of me. I would just run the other way and take my shitty attitude with me. One day I realised just how terrible I was treating him and another gentleman that had some very quirky thoughts about life. I was treating them with disdain. How dare I? How did I for a moment convince myself that they were less than I? Really, that is despicable of me.

There and then, I made up my mind to listen and, as an exercise for myself, to love them. To treat them as equal fellow humans, in pain.

In all my "good for humanity" talk, here is me, avoiding these men. I felt the conviction of God to be kind. I made myself be with them for one hour each morning and evening.

I sat and listened to them. I became so in love with the simple process of closing my mouth and opening my ears. The wonders behind their beliefs, what a beauty there is in that simplicity of thought. I have to say that one hour each morning and night turned rapidly into playing games, talking trash – literally, understanding life on the streets, but simply it taught me to hold a person's heart in my hands and just breathe care into them, but no one told me I would learn twice as much from them. Isn't it interesting, in retrospect, that with all the utmost respect, he had been thrown to the street, like trash, and yet he was adamant to re-purpose any trash he saw around him. That reality rips my heart apart. He found more value in trash.

When I left, I was terribly sad. I found myself so choked up at the departure I had to return a few days later to say hello, only to discover that I was too late. They were gone. I only have the memory of their most gracious, kind words to me, the one who unjustly judged them before I left. "Love and Light", one said. "Love and Light" as he held my praying hands in his. What a beautiful human connection.

How, I ask you, did I so oddly fall into this situation thinking I needed to do good by them and be kind when in turn learned the error of my ways, and they are the ones who had the lesson for me. By God's grace, that is human connection.

I had no reason to expect anything out of that encounter, but I have to tell you, it has changed my life for the better. I would love us all to experience that kindness, giving and receiving.

So if hurt people, hurt people..... maybe loved people, love people?

Make real connections.

God bless and keep you all.

Joelle.

If you desire to share anything with me, please, by all means, feel free to email. I would love to hear your reactions.

throughscreamingwhispers@gmail.com

REVIEW

by Regina Gerlach

'BE QUIET AND LISTEN'

*I*n this book Joelle Johnson is sharing her personal experience and insight into what it is like to live with complex PTSD. *Through Screaming Whispers, published in 2022,* is a compiled work of prose and poems expressing and voicing the author's experience of tremendous psychological and emotional terror re-experienced in her adult life.

Joelle Johnson invites the reader to *be quiet and listen* and presents with an aspiration to raise awareness and to help *"people to understand"* the multi-faceted impact complex PTSD has.

The author has been confronted with a judging and misunderstanding community as she had to come to an understanding of her trauma herself. Her poems capture and express the complexity of her experience over many years, in fact six years to date. In a very artistic way Joelle Johnson describes her battle with the awakening childhood trauma memories.

This anthropology is showcasing how writing, in particular poetry not only helps voicing trauma, but also utilises a poetic language to grasp the essence of human experience.

I can only echo and encourage the reader to choose wisely the time and place where you are going to read this seven-chapter anthropology. Indeed, "*this book is not for the faint of heart*". Choose discernment and your wise mind and heart as you are reading and understanding what Joelle Johnson and so many other individuals are living with.

In the middle of their life *memories from childhood* arise: the past becomes present, and life becomes unbearable. In the first chapter *CHASING BUNNIES* Joelle Johnson provides us with a personal introduction describing the beginning of six years of re-lived trauma reinforcing terror, fear, shame, guilt, and despair. A question is raised by the author: "W*ould you prefer not to know?*" As I am contemplating this question, I am engaging much deeper with the author and their trauma narrative. And I realise this is a question that neither the author nor a survivor, friend, peer or professional can eas-ily answer. This question is adding an addi-tional layer to the work through trauma. It creates distance and invites a much deeper view into life and its challenges.

In *THE RECKONING*, chapter two, we learn about the overwhelming impact of trauma (drowning into the trauma): paralys-ing and demobilising. *Two ears are needed* to hear and to unpack the trauma with the help of a psychologist. It is like the hero's journey by Joseph Campbell who describes the stage of *initiation*, to embrace the chal-lenge and to seek a mentor in doing so. I don't think what is described in this book can be labelled as *challenge* though. It must be called what it is, TRAUMA, CPTSD (Complex Posttraumatic Stress Disorder), however. Facing the terror with professional help often can result in being overwhelmed and traumatised by overwhelm itself. In this chapter, the author voices not only their experience of risk to self and depression whilst facing all the memories and emotional disturbances. And as if this would not have been enough, Joelle Johnson wakes up to a mental health crisis that is struggling to cope with the demand of mental health concerns. *Be quiet and listen. The* poems expressively capture the essence of the author's experience whilst embracing the trauma, outside and inside *THE MADHOUSE.*

In *THE GOOD, THE BAD, THE UGLY,* chapter three, the question "W*ould you prefer to not know?"* is revisited by the author. In the quest for life, there seems to be a notion of hope. In her attempt to contemplate this question she writes "... *suffering draws me to the cross ... discover the comfort of*

Christ ... he understands me, even when others don't." The notion of *forgiveness* is mentioned and considered for the first time. It may feel too soon, too radical, and too quick. I don't know. Every human being that has experienced what the author describes in their book has different internal and external resources as well as different capacities available. Nevertheless, the author describes their aloneness and isolation: "W*ho to talk to if nobody understands?*". Exhaustion is expressed and it is finding its way into the poems. Exhaustion that comes with a desperate call for a way out in *ENTER THE DOORS*. And then there is the wish to be "*taken away*" and in *A POET'S CONSIDERATION* the further depth of the trauma is revealed. As a reader you may feel taken through the turmoil, it feels chaotic and disorganised in the order of healing. And yet, this is part of what it feels like. A mixture of hope and forgiveness as well as hopelessness and despair. And for a moment refuge in forgiveness takes place.

Listen to the *THREE IN ONE*, chapter four. The Greek word for trauma is *traumatisks*; it means *wound*. There is perhaps no better description of the hurt and psychological wound than trauma. The previous chapters (1-3) capture the experiences, reactions, and impact of the author's trauma. This chapter captures the visceral expression and intense felt sense of emotional and psychological trauma. Joelle Johnson talks about the *"three in one"* that are affected and part of the trauma narrative. She describes this with distance from an observer perspective as she is using the third person whilst describing their appearances. Please be prepared this part of the book is certainly not for the fainthearted. So, please take a moment and pause. You may want to ground yourself and check whether it is the right time to continue reading. This chapter is quite complex, but also contained. I appreciate the author taking skilful care in the amount, style, and content.

PLEASE NO MORE, chapter five, Joelle Johnson calls for a *rest*. She expresses her exhaustion quite vividly in *MY BROKEN HEART*. This poem can be seen as a summary of memories and the attempts to make sense, to repair and to heal. This ongoing search for identity *"and all that I have left is something I am not"* and the need to find a ground to stand on to be freed. And yet, the poem reveals there seems no resource available anymore. Chapter five and no answers. In *WHY*, the search for THE answer fails in a way. Can there ever be any sense made of why this happened to Joelle Johnson. And yet, it offers to see something new in the old. Maybe forming a new relationship with six years of relived trauma? I wonder what difference it would make if there would be a consistent sense of identity - grounded, stable, and integrated. This is something the author might elaborate on in her autobiography. And as she describes in her next chapter, mindfulness might be able to help.

This chapter feels like a jump. *MAKING PEACE* marks the ending of a series of prose and poetry. You might ask, is chapter six all about hope or is it about giving in? *"I am moving forward now"* doesn't mean to forget, or to give in. There is change shining through this chapter including a sense of authority, courage, and willingness to continue the exploration of trauma in a different way. Joelle Johnson decided to embrace her trauma and is now ready for a new approach. Coming back to Joseph Campbell's *The Hero's Journey*, it seems Joelle returns with more insight, more clarity in certain parts. The trauma is not resolved, and a question arises *will it ever be?* Joelle Johnson has been through hell that is for sure. She has offered the reader an insight into her world and flagged a few possible soothing and comforting ways to be with or out of trauma, i.e., engaging in therapy, being comforted by Christ, *"humming the way to be"*. But is that enough to live with the past that still feels like it is in the present when memories surface?

Time will tell, as well as the new approach that Joelle Johnson has embraced and taken. In *BRING HER HOME* she shares with us what the "*little one*" inside needs. And what the adult one Joelle Johnson needs "*my desire has only ever been, one with you!*"

Concluding with a story about two men and a significant lesson to be learned. This ending is a demonstration of what the author is attempting to achieve. "*Listen ... became in love with the simple process of closing my mouth and opening my ears*" is an invitation to all of us. Listen and take others seriously, without judgment, without measure.

In this book, the author invites us into their inner world, into what it feels like to go through trauma. Joelle Johnson does this in a very artistic, skilful, and insightful way. She is mastering the art of expression without exposing the reader to each detail of the trauma itself. The author has chosen to voice their trauma in the form of poetry that is revealing the intention that gives birth to clear words. Words that are no longer suppressed in the silence and pain that was caused in the past.

This book is an act of balance, offering us to connect with the multi-facets of trauma and its phenomena, being drawn into the pain of terror as well as the tiny glimmer of hope. There is a way out, or should I say a way to live with it or without. The author describes the many attempts and ways to understand their trauma, its echoing and rippling impact in their life in each second. However, the search inside, outside and the discoveries within this, is ongoing work.

Hearing stories from our peers can be very inspiring and helpful. It is encouraging, normalising, and acknowledging what individuals go through if they have experienced complex trauma. *"This is a cupcake version",* the author says because her *"set of traumas are so deep that it is not wise to share with non-professionals".* And therefore, she makes it accessible to the reader who might have experienced this type of trauma, or who might be a friend of someone who has gone through this. She articulates trauma in a creative way and creates an alignment between the victims of trauma. It also reveals not only the face, impact, and effect of trauma on someone's life, it also reveals its ever presence.

Joelle Johnson has carefully chosen a collection of poems to protect the reader "*a cupcake version*". If this book is a "*cupcake version*" you can only imagine what the cake might look like.

One way to integrate trauma is through self-compassion, mindfulness, forgiveness and radical acceptance of memories and strong emotions (in addition to therapy, not replacing therapy). This work requires guts and courage. It requires a safer connection to engage in the process, to feel heard and understood. Joelle Johnson encourages every one of us to first "*be quiet and listen*", to be aware of our judgments and to disengage from them, to open our heart and to listen from within. And even if we can do this, it will be still challenging to fully understand. And even as a professional in the field of trauma-informed and trauma-sensitive work it is at times challenging to comprehend what someone is going through when they relive their trauma. So, for us as professionals, we too need to *be quiet and listen.*

Regina Gerlach, Clinical Psychologist and Mindfulness Practitioner, Perth, Western Australia.

ACKNOWLEDGEMENTS

The mental health industry in Australia continues to improve each year, I suspect through the workings of some key personnel fighting for the voiceless.

I have seen all manner and forms of health care workers represented in mental hospitals and have endured disdain from some who do not comprehend the driving forces of mental health, or the poor souls have had to put up with so much, for so long, that they have given up.

Very rarely do you see patients in mental health facilities who have come in before the point of absolute desperation? Instead, they are sometimes dangerous, out of their minds, homeless, friendless, and to the point where society has almost thrown them away. It can become a highly volatile situation. You also have professionals who treat the same patients repeatedly because the system is failing, lacking or too expensive. It is a highly complex problem, but our government does its best. But it could do better.

I have met many heroes in this field during my stays. This acknowledgement is for the cleaners, the tea lady and the community volunteers hidden behind the scenes that you see every day and always chat to. These treasures store aside cookies or keep back extra sandwiches for those long screaming nights; they bring you a smile every morning, and hello, they get to know you just as a person because they genuinely care.

Special mention to the nurses in these acute wards. They have to tolerate unimaginable things on any given day at work and yet stay ready to battle them down.

Inside their chest, beats the hearts of lions!

The most touching moment I had during hospitalisation was this beautiful African Nurse holding onto me, trying to contain the desperate shaking my body was enduring through the ravages of fear. Her sweet smell filtered through while singing Amazing Grace, with tears dropping down her cheeks. Her name was Precious. She had no idea of my troubles; she just loved me because that was her job as a nurse and a sister in Christ.

REFERENCES

Mr Paul Ward

MPsych (Clinical) BBus

Warwick Psychological Services

https://wps.support/paul-ward/

admin@wps.support

Mrs Regina Gerlach

Clinical Psychologist

Accredited Mindfulness Practitioner

Mindfulness2 be Psychology

https://www.mindfulness2be.com/reginagerlach psychology

reginagerlachpsychology@gmail.com

If I were to name a single "therapy" as far as progress and repair, in addition to traditional therapy that I could recommend, it would be Mindfulness-Based Cognitive Therapy.

For further information and training regarding mindfulness and its treatment for Clinical Depressive Disorders, I urge you to follow the below links and obtain some clinical data to help.

However, if you are in Western Australia, please get in touch with Regina Gerlach for information on courses.

Mindful Based Cognitive Therapy

- Access MBCT
- International register of accredited MBCT teachers

  https://www.accessmbct.com/

- BAMBA - British Association of Mindfulness-Based Approaches

  Information about
  Teaching and Guidelines Standards pdf.

  https://bamba.org.uk/wp-content/uploads/2020/01/GPG-for-Teaching-Mindfulness-Based-Courses-BAMBA.pdf

Lightning Source UK Ltd.
Milton Keynes UK
UKHW050252070422
401071UK00008BA/167/J

9 780645 426526